Poetry and Assorted Pieces of Clothing

PETER VEALEY

CHIPMUNKA CLASSICS

CHIPMUNKA CLASSICS

All rights reserved, no part of this publication may be reproduced by any means, electronic, mechanical photocopying, documentary, film or in any other format without prior written permission of the publisher.

Published by
Chipmunkapublishing
United Kingdom

http://www. chipmunkaclassics.co.uk

Copyright © Peter Vealey 2015

ISBN   978-1-78382-210-2

Preface

This is my third book of poetry titled, "Poetry and Assorted Pieces of Clothing"
Written throughout my life, hopes, sojourn and failures.
A mix of variety of places and people.
The Political, the social, the animal in me.
Dedicated to Poetry Kind and Human Kind.
Sixty Years of Dreaming of a better world.
The most general and true to my spirit
Of loving humanity,
Yet without a clue where to find it.

Acknowledgements

Gillian Bergh, for the invaluable editing and consultation on this collection of poems.

To everyone out there and assorted ensembles, however briefly you came into my life. You made it all possible, providing the necessary colour and diversion to my soul.

Biography

Peter is sixty something new,
Rebellious as ever in spirit and
The proud recipient of the
2014 Rethink Pringle Award for Poetry.
Here within is his Third Book of Poetry,
And probably the book
He was always
Meant to write.

Alcohol

I used to hang my head
Like Pinocchio at the bar.
Sneering down a long dark road.
Thinking I knew better.
Observational blues,
 Just observational blues.
I used to go everywhere,
But I was never, ever cool,
Or hip at the joint.
I used to think I was
Above it all.
While trying to empathize.
But now it seems
The yawning reality
Of those days tells me -
I knew myself, oh no-no!
Only when I was
Sneering, jeering and drowning.
Down a dark, dark road.
Hanging down
Over a bar.
Like a tired snake.
Waiting for the newsreel,
Of the jumped-up fake.

Alone in the Car wash

Alone in the car wash.
I feel splendidly calm for once.
It's raining outside.
You know, some people
Are frightened of these devices,
Still I am
Alone in the car wash,
As usual.
The brushes bend my mirror
Inwards.
The rusted car ariel
I cannot remove,
Rattles on the bonnet,
As the journey of the wash progresses.
Alone in the car wash.
I feel I would solve
All the world's ills.
Till the process inevitably ends
My haven,
And I exit
My bunker of safety.
Leaving my car.
All the anxieties of life,
Flood back.
To a mere mortal,
In the grey pouring rain
Of an English summer.

A Poetry Reading

A flabby forgettable face
Kills the muted, unnatural silence.
She laughs timidly
 In childlike embarrassment.
The famous poet stares
At the ceiling,
Trying to conceal his yawndom.
Next to me they wonder
Why I do not clap automatically.
The safe enclosed evening is programmed for
Proceeds to the ……..

A Precise Art?

That place we were.
How right it seemed then.
The feel of each other.

A precise art.
Flawed by time.
So now sadly out of
Rhyme and communication.
Memories captured somewhere in time.

A hidden pain,
an unrecognised crime
Of betrayal.
Who's to blame?
This precise art of lovin' is never known.
.
Two minds in synchronicity,
Or in different worlds of relativity?
The on-going reality of life.
What was that?
Oh, just a scientist's thesis on relationships.

A precise art,
or another fool's falling love dart.

Cleansed

The bleached faces of
Parents and children,
Coming out
Of a Stortford Sunday morning
Ritual.
Cleansed.
All we need is this momentary resurgence of
Hope.
What a pity
All the poverty and murder
Still goes on unabated.
However we'll (regardless) collect
(And in time forget).
For at the end of the day
We're all glad to shut our
Doors to the pain.

Conversations in a Barbers'.

Conversations
In a Barbers'.
How difficult that
Must be.
Chit-chat that
Doesn't grate, crosses borders
Still demonises
In a populist way.
Chit-chat,
Flim-flam
Sport, the latest scandal
All will be revealed
But not here.
Conversations
In a Barbers'.
Getting on with the public.
The ultimate challenge?
That faces us all.
Chit-chat
Or face the sack.
Chit and no chat
Nose to the wheel.
Save all that unnecessary spiel.
And hey presto
The gold watch
Re-appears.
Headlines in the paper reading queue
Said
"Man found looking
For his fate"

A cheery bye-bye
Flows off the customer's tongue.
Can't be late,
Sails out of the window,
In the time
It took to cut my hair.

Daddy Longlegs

You're in my urban world.

In the countryside.
Lame on the bottom of the bath.
Daddy Longlegs.
I look to see signs of life.
Unsteady, slight movements are observed.
Pick up precarious.
I am seriously
Worried.
You will not survive
My clay hands.
Daddy Longlegs.
With a wish and a prayer,
You are gone.
Out of my window for
A song.
Released to your world.
Do not come back here.
It is not safe!

December

December...
Choking on petrol fumes,
Weaned on out of date tunes.
Christmas sharks,
Making pneumonia in the park.
Sleeping people, resembling logs.
The nights' indefatigable cogs.
Chugging away on sorry souls.
December...
Delivering yourself
At doors.
Tiresome end of year
Chores.
Young and old literally dying
For a good smile.
Paler than a virgin's sweet, sweet
Buttock.
Who's that face
Nosing suspicious.
From that so cold house.
Shut the curtains tight.
Your world's dormant
For yet another night.
Blue icy light spiralling
Skywards.
Forever is your earth.

Dissipation

Dissipation.
Persuasion, Elevation, Escapism.
All things are possible, yet nothing
Is as clear.
As you would want for an answer.
A new friend looks one way,
Others hide in 'soaps' or alcohol.
Dissipation, Revelation.
All is nearly here.
Yet nothing remains certain.
A changing tapestry in an unchanging world.
The meaning of life,
It was just over there!
I saw it scuttle round the alley.
Could have sworn it would always
Keep me warm.
Why is there ice running through my veins
Today?

Down the Road of Play

We've all run along
Down this road of play.
Today,
All to say,
There's nothing there.
Old ghosts of no repair.
The illness is over.
The soothsayer said the teddy bear
Is told to stand and stare.
There's nothing there,
it's fair to say.
It was a while ago.
You told me so.
There's nothing there.
Just old paranoia,
Circle in a square.
There's nothing there.
What's to compare.
Fools on a carousel square.
Horses going up'n down,
Waiting for the clown
To dare say nothing at all,
Or is there?

Dreamboats

You were a passing ship
In the night.
At once a momentary delight,
(With a shadow of a fright).
The free untamed spirit of youth!
Dangling free.
Scaring the old man in me.
Someone said like "fatal attraction",
One could be drawn in.
Gossips whispered,
'Better to stay on the straight and narrow,'
Might have sounded more honest
From all yous.
You became overnight,
Someone I would probably
Never see again.
My attraction to you,
Not physical,
Only intellectual.
Such things don't form
Lasting lust.

Everything is Perfect in his Garden

Everything is perfect in his garden.
Well the round the back, he's working on.
But who sees it, apart from me?
 It's as tidy as his mind.
Everything is perfect in his garden.
The work ethic runs oh so strong.
He's really a regular guy,
Democratic as an autocratic
Could ever be.
A one-eyed man,
Not really searching for
The wider span.
Got the grass cut to
Wimbledon standard.
The flowers growing in line,
There's no "wildness" here.
Emotions are kept in check
By routine.
And life is performed
At a brisk pace
Until he dies.

Falling in Love (is as Dangerous as it Gets)

Falling in love is as dangerous as it gets.
The pain, the heartache, the inevitable fret.
Used to worry that I had,
No new love left to find.
But the fall from grace,
Is so often unkind.
A fool's platter of one.
Young, old and everyone under the sun.
Falling in love is as dangerous as it gets.
The emotions of tumble and upset.
You must not ever forget
(Or really regret).
Falling in love is as dangerous as it gets.
The pain, the heartache,
The inevitable angst and fret drip.
I remember that feeling so well.
And sometimes if it's worth the dwelling
Upon such trifles as these
If one feeling never turns to two entwined.
It just will not do,
Never do.

Februarys

Each February is coming and going
So fast.
I'm writing in this tiny room.
The world seems colder and greyer than
I've ever known.
Another war is what the old fools say.
We need to bleed.
Thirty years and more is far too long,
With this uneasy tension
Called peace.
Old wounds, new blood spilt,
Reasons to be found- will be.
I guess I'm just a no-good pacifist
To you, old soldier,
But to me
Born to live should be,
Born to die naturally.
And each February like this
Doesn't feel
Like the threshold
Of a new spring.
Love songs on the radio ease
Like bad drugs,
That in the end
Won't overcome wars.

Feed my Ego

Feed my Ego
I send my money to you,
To feed my ego.
See my words in print,
See my life in crisis,
(For all to see).
Run to the waters of time.
Let the angry wolf, cry tears of joy.
For the feeding of the ego,
Insatiable and empty,
Is the leading of the horse.
And the unjust run wild,
On the lack of balance,
These dark times.

Fluidity

People are everywhere you go.
Pottering from A to B.
The fabric of a nation.
People are everywhere you may be.
They can nearly always see.
Pottering from to and fro,
Always dying to 'go'.
Looking for the man 'in the know'.
Eccentric, pedantic,
A million varieties.
-Always looking for more.
Never certain where to go.
People are everywhere,
On the river, down the lane.
Pottering from B to A.

(For a) Misnomer

She wafted in
Like a sea-breeze,
And made me feel
A little less than impossible
(To be with).
Like a summers misty morning,
Too gentle
For any malice or forethought.
A time of easy beginnings,
Charmed losses.
Yet barely-heard sighs.

Front Windows and Appearance

Looking out of front windows
For two and a half years.
Has got you close to tears
So many times.
Appearance is all.
Never let it be seen
That you are
Struggling.
Front windows,
Knitting and chewing nails
Aerobics and appearances
Of making a go of life,
To your parents.
Front windows and appearances.
Looking out of front windows
For two and a half years,
Has got you close to tears
So many times.
Appearance is all.
Never let it be seen
That you are
Struggling.
Front windows,
Knitting and chewing nails,
Aerobics and appearances,
Of making a go of life,
To your parents.

GLORY, GORY WAR

In the world of the
Glory gory war.
Debate is stifled, muted
By chest-puffed medals of valour.
Displayed so prominently in a uniformity of misinformation
Of the real exit plan.
In the land of Gory glory war.
Justified indignation
Is commonplace
For the fallen, silent dead.
Yet truth
Is led away,
Crying and mourning
In the land of the glory gory war.
Debate is nowhere.
Revenge and retribution rage always
Among
Those follies of insolence and wanton betrayal
Regret is shown
The back door quietly.
In the land of the
Glory, gory war.
Justified war is always
The greatest deceiver of humanity.
Justified war always
The greatest reason for its continuing popularity.
Amongst the beaten down patriot
In the ghost lands
Of the glory, gory war.

Go Down and Drink the Tranquil Seas.

Go down and drink the tranquil seas
Of a million rocky coves,
Stand up on a high point,
See the motionless deceptive sea
And a few unhurried looking boats
Like directionless targets.
Clamber about and hurt your feet.
Walk on the wild hill
Exhausted lie still,
Sleep the afternoon away.
It`s all part of time,
A circling rhyme,
Let the wind
Have its own way.
Gorse bushes and stony fields
Heather and weeds.
A serene arrogant
Hawk flies.
Soaring and
Dipping in the wind.

"Going Public"

We put up a poster
Designed to delete,
And keep you from coming
With its formal elitist title.
It was bound to prevent you
From opening your doors.
Though the "Culture" on the poster,
Was a sign of desperation
Of how badly we needed
"You!"
Heard my Bed n'Breakfast landlady
Epitomise in awkward floundering-
"I don't understand poetry,
So I don't bother to read it"
But poets are everywhere
And mostly kept
Rather nowhere.
In stark-lighted seated halls
Through limited evenings
Of intense over- exposure.
Curious creatures,
All the same.
But we like everyday pursuits you know!
Is it all a designed plan
To keep you from me,
Or you from them inside?
Musicians seem in the main
To find their direction
But poets
As I saw here

Are isolated, journeying souls,
Meeting in toilets n' bars.
Because the formal receptions
"Are more a P.R. exercise
To get the theatre"
And the poetry?
 Well, Maybe next year! ……..

Gristle to the Mill

Sunset scorches the shiny gates
Of a school.
Blistering tears of a
Passing summers night.
Gristle to the mill.
Driving over the hill
Metronomic motions on
Patrol still.
Radio stories of
Old ghosts and feudal wars.
Just gristle to the mill.
Stand by the road
Of the overblown overkill.
Sunset by the trees
Pressing down on
The longest night
Of Kingdom Come.
(Just gristle to the mill),
Still and Evermore.

Harvestsong

The last apple in the garden
Fell unnoticed,
While I was away,
Making hay.
From August to December.
From rain to mid-never.
So cold as
'Shiver me timbers'.
The last apple
Tasted bland and damp.
The fruit of all God,
For all to see.
Nature's harvest replenishing
Wild and ever free.
The last apple was mine,
For the first time,
Falling from August
To gone Christmas morn on.
From sunshine, rain and fall
 Through winter's seemingly (forever).
Without a snowdrop to recall.

I Fall Off the Wagon Sometimes

I fall off the wagon sometimes.
I beat up myself
 Oh my!
I fall off the wagon sometimes.
I may gloat that the warrior
Is in retreat.
But the war isn't over
And the lover is still at the door.
Insistent as any mistress would be.
I beat myself up badly
On the illusionary crime
That all is healed,
And time was always mine.
I fall off the wagon sometimes.
Looking for the holes
In the wall of life (to never ever see.)
They were always there.
(And meant to be so!)
I fell off the wagon
Again tonight,
Waiting for the
Silk seductress siren
Of past midnight
To come howling
For my surrender.

IF I GET STARTED

If I get started
What can go wrong?
If I get started
Where will it go?
Only time will show
If I get started
The night will fall
Before sun comes up,
And you will know
Who I am.
If I get started
Love will tumble
Hate will rise
If I get started
Only violence prevails.
If I get started
The genie's out of the bottle.
The darkness of night
Will always be so
Right (and white).
You'll always
Believe it was destiny
To destroy all before us.

I'm a Dreamer (In a Dreamless World)

I am a dreamer and proud to be so.
Saw a shadow cross a room last night.
There's more to life than your vision will allow.
Life and death,

Who we are and where we go.
Rolling conversation of instant trepidation.
Would I be loud and assertive?
Directionless as an empty vessel!
But maybe that's just bias on my part.
Guess I am a dreamer in a dreamless world.

Image (IS ALL)

You got to look like this,
You got to have that.
You got to go forward,
You must not turn back.
Image is all.
Your image can be too mumsy and small.
Image has got to be cool,
At any cost.
What you can't be seen to do
Is to have lost out
To Father Time.
What a terrible crime!
You're so passé
You got to still want to play.
The road must never look
Less than a fresh horizon.
Brand new rain,
Coming down this morn
On this tired Old Island.
Image is all.
And we can't recall,
That we used to be,
Not so long ago,
Caring, tolerant and free.

Into the Ether

You brushed by
Brisk and anonymous.
With a breezy 'hello!'
Flakier than I like to remember
(Or believe).
Didn't believe a word,
Of who you were or are.
Cleared the air
Maybe.
But do I trust you?
No!
Soon you were gone.
Back into the ether,
As if we had
Never happened.

Just Another Suicide Song

Every word I write here
Is a scar.
Of the pain.
Living without your love.
Like blood from a gashed arm.
Accidents are part of life.
And the wounds of relationships
Never get much easier to bear.
Every word I wrote today
Was a scar.
Of the hurt of you
 not wanting me back.
And the blood from a gashed broken heart.
Are there for all to see.
Accidents are part of life.
And the skeletons of relationships
Never get any easier to handle.

Lately Part 2

The bits don't fit anymore.
The calls are response driven,
Knee-jerk almost.
Not instinctive now.
I still like you,
And that makes it difficult.
Can see why we were a unit.
But also,
The mechanics of a puzzle are now
Flawed by absence.
I feel I am teetering on near
Resentment.
Drifting into a decayed death
Of a self-motivated recovery.
Wishing you were still in my life,
And not a fading memory.

Little Ripples

Little ripples
On a tranquil sea.
Are they really that calm?
Can I cross them
Like a bump in the road?
Do I find the strength
(Like in youthful naivety?)
To speed on through.
Till one overtakes me
In my mind.
Little ripples.
They scare me so.
I keep swimming, day by day.
Eyes just above the ripples.
Coming, coming relentlessly.
Little ripples, little ripples.
Be kind to my
Mind!
The salt water relaxation
Is taking me away
From earthly cares.
But how many more ripples
Can I surmount?
Before I give up,
And just become a memory
In people's minds.

Losing things

I`ve been losing things,
All my life.
Cameras, people, towels, phones
Lovers, friends.
I am always anxious
For the postman to call.
Losing things.
Waiting for a mirror to fall.
Too suspicious to walk
Under the ladder of it all.
Losing things.
Yet can't grasp it all.
Losing things.
Objects, losing things.
I've been losing touch.
Finding so much
In everything.
Losing things.

Love springs

Loving is not the easiest thing
 In the world to handle.
But writing has always been
A source of joy,
And flows naturally.
Although I try,
From time to time to
Tap it.
It then never runs at all.
And loving all you
Has been the source of the fall.

Lounge Lizard

I'm a lounge lizard
Almost wizened.
Oh so smooth.
As smooth as
A crocodile
Running through the water
Of mud.
I'm a lounge lizard
Waiting on a cruise evening.
Loose feeling,
Lounge lizard.
Smooth as a rat in
A pack.
Lounge lizard.
So, so wizened.
Neon nites.
Hanging on high down,
Upside down.
Waiting to lie.
Lounge lizard.
Leathery
Like a banker,
Waiting for the war
To anchor.

Mediocrity or Purpose Divine

A poem does not look much,
Just scribbled on any scrap
Of available paper or tissue.
Put it into print,
Give it a title.
All can be revealed
In an instant.
Mediocrity or purpose divine.
A poem does not always
Seem relevant,
Just scribbled with
Errors and adjustments.
Crossed out lines and words.
Does not do it justice.
Put it into print,
Give it a name or two.
All will unfold,
In an instant.
How pompous it all seems,
This little ol' poem divine
That started off as solely mine.
In a terrible dream.
I escaped to find reality.

MISSING

I am always missing
Trains in dreams.

I am always missing
Boats (in life).

Moody

I have a dark side to me.
That looks for the soul to see.
I have a heart,
That will not let the
Heartless and feckless
Feel nothing at all.
I have a clinical edge,
For seeing beyond the
Easy and shallow.
I have a dark side to me.
That wants the bad
To be held at sea.
Where their pain cannot
Grow endlessly.
I can be moody and grumpy
About the state of humankind.
If I can give,
Why can't you?
(See the oncoming rain)
I have a dark side to me
looking for the soul to see,
Beyond the easy and shallow.
I have a cold eye,
For the aggressive and unkind.
Their message is as poor as at
Any time of this world.

My Car (Divorce)

Today I collected papers
Posted papers.
All that's left of my car.
Pieces of papers,
Lonely papers.
They didn't tell the story
Of the bliss of you.
of music and travelling.
In fact they didn't
Tell a soul,
Anything else than,
You weren't alive anymore,
But in my memory.
Lonely papers
On the road to nowhere.
For pen pushers
And bureaucrats
To feel important
One more day
Than never …….

Painting Pictures

Painting pictures
Framing walls,
Flaming calls of no light.
Painting pictures,
Stalling for time.
I am always painting
Pictures.
Waiting for a clearer dawn.
Oh painting pictures!
Jumping off rhythms
Of heart and road.
The lone day draws in
Weary.
Like a sea on umpteenth
Return to land.
Painting pictures, just
Painting pictures
For all to see.

Passing the Baton.

It had to end.
We had all this.
So absorbed in all our comforts.
Photos, framed memories,
Holidays, various locations.
It lasted longer than
Either of us,
Secretly dared to hope.
Now we are just someone
Else's memories.
Isn't that the way,
Time immemorial.
We all think we
Are more important
Because we outlived 'you'.
How sad!
Feel the quality,
Not the width.

Plants are Ripe

Plants are ripe.
The night without return.
Distant images scatter to form and dissipate
In the fogs of the minds' willing forgetfulness.
No sound to break
The glassless darkness.
Weary messages relayed effortlessly
By a stark brain.
Plants are over ripe
(And soon to die).
Lilting songs are there in the
Distance between my ears and
Reality.
Voices clatter, scarce and syncopated
Harsh, unfeeling
Did they love you?
Did you really ever love anyone?

Playing

Blowing trees,
From pillar to post
Careless wisp and sway.
Ancient songs of night and day.
Blowing trees,
From post to pillar.
The wearied, yet fresh soothsayer.
Witchdoctor on high
Of fears yet to come.
Blowing trees!
The sway of old worlds,
Unravelling like gales
Out to sea.

Pushing up Daisies

I looked at a garden today
Of someone else's home,
And thought
I don't want ever to be
Pushing up Daisies.
Find my soul somewhere else.
A clear blue sea,
A bright snow-kissed morn,
Anywhere
But
Pushing up daisies.
I am not there,
You are not here.
The world is an illusionary
Pact of distortion.
And the players
Just left
For the furthest star from here.

School Dinners

I removed a meal
From a microwave,
And it took me back
So many years.
To school dinners.
The order, the
Discipline of
Rows and rows of rigid seats.
The awful smell of
Fright.
Pervading my shy heart
Of a boyhood.
School dinners.
Scottish Country Dancing
In the shiny polished hall,
Girls preening and jigging purposefully.
Boys gushing at their awkward moves,
Amidst childish titters
Scorned on
By hawkish country maid frowns.

Scream

Haystacks and Augusts,
And country lanes.
Woodland swooping birds.
Winding roads and pubs.
Rivers, bridges, waterfalls.
Cornfields and bubbling streams.
Willow trees and rivers in bloom.
July is my lover.
Blossom pink flowers
Floating away,

Bang!
And the dream is over.

Silhouettes (Maddened Clown)

I used to promote me,
But no one could see
Was the man to be?

They were always
Travelling in their own
Universes,
Oblivious to their
Patent reverses.

Fears that a mind cloistered
Tears of self-pitiful pity,
Was I?

Silhouettes of ancient bigots.
I like a spectre of a
Maddened Clown.
Leave pictures I can't explain.

Sketches

You always remind me of other people,
But never remind me of you.

Sockets

Everything comes down
To sockets.
You're either getting into
Or withdrawing.
Painfully, recklessly or carefully.
Power, sex, money,
Amid connections.
Whatever you do,
However hard you strive
For your nirvana.
Sockets, sockets!
It all begins and ends
On joining together
In passionate, fresh loving innocence.
Only to end
Often years later.
In affairs of renewing vigour,
In search of
Fresher socketry.

Song for humanity

We are virgin flowers in the spring.
We are lovers in afterglow (don't you know).
We are nights without end.
Sleeping round the bend of the harsh winter.
We are soul-diers of the world.
See our colours unfurl,
Slow or last.
Disintegrate or pass.
We are livers of the love dream,
Of a half-forgotten, sunken scheme.
We are fliers without air,
Scarred souls beyond repair.
We are virgin flowers in the spring.
Lovers of a (ceaseless) quest.
For unordained pastures of joy.
We are breakers on the pools.
Benders of the rules.
Fakirs on cushioned stools.
Foolish, fodder failures
For the unawakened cause.

Still-born (Fools' Paradise)

Our relationship
Is as perfect,
As a still-born child.
Never dared to be
Touched
Ever again,
For fear of
Revealing
It was never
Perfect.
Only in our minds' eye
Of each other.

Sundancer

New weekends
Come and too soon gone.
Are only faded fragments.
Distorted.
In your face.
A life aborted.
Youth was ours.
Like everyone,
The garden party
Was always
Food left over.
Never as good
As in your mind.
Mothers' tired frown,
When the night
Had passed.
At all the clearing up
To be done.
Next year we'll plan
It better in
January letters.
Evenings spent poorly
Walking out your weary old setter.

Swooping with the Swallows

I was looking for some
Calm n' solace,
Amidst the shimmering
Fields and rushes.
I'd often admired from my window.
Took myself out for a while
From the grim grind of
Daily woes.
Swooping with the swallows.
Resting my head on Mother Earth
One tree in a field.
Thought of all the worlds n' faces
Come and gone
And how I must always
Guard from lingering
To an old tired song.
Swooping with the swallows.
 Dive n' Soar,
Hunt n' roar
But never
Be thought of as bore.
Swooping with the swallows.
To take a fresh perspective.
Of you and yore.

Talking to Yourself Blues

The phone's not going
To ring you know!
The clock ticks your life away.
On a sunny autumnal day in the country.
Damn!
How I wish,
I had that book of addresses
To console myself
Of friendlier days.
But that phone's not going to ring oh!
I've got to go out
And bring about.
Some changes without
To within.

Temporary Vehicles

We are all temporary vehicles
On a road to Jerusalem.
Temporary vehicles.
In time of sun.
We all run to fields of gold.
We are all temporary vehicles
In this theatre of dreams.
Falling through this
Stage of fright.
Temporary vehicles.
On a road to ruin,
Of age and decay
Temporary vehicles
In this body of sin,
True soul of love
Lives within.

The Afternoon Song

Sit in the sun on the chair light-blue,
Let the dogs bark.
The cats fight and play.
Get some air,
Some colour in your face.
Put some music here.
Slow, sad guitar strumming away.
Read a book,
Sleep a little.
Get a tan on your arms and hand,
Appreciate the journey is here today.

The Departure Lounge

Many times,
I have been near the departure lounge.
Never knew the how or why.
Only too near tears to cry.
Time to leave.
Clichés on your sleeve.
Ready to be 'sold'.
Like cards up, an armful ready.
The departure lounge.
What is this place?
The only sensible option!
Many times,
I could have gone
Rather than see and play out
Bitter endings.
The departure lounge!
A better place to be looking at
From a comfortable view
Than actually arrive at.

The Envelope

You are doin' stuff
Together.
Like we did.
(She did, he did)
Now is then.
Then is tomorrow.
Words are useless.
You're in the
Here and now.
I am your yesterday.
You must know I loved you.
Oh
And we are in
That envelope called "our time".

The Funeral

It passed
Without a murmur
"A very brave man"
Many said.
Many local people
Were there,
Like so many others
Recollecting thoughts and memories.
A life gone,
 A life that had
The worth of anything
To be judged by whom?
An ordeal to get through,
Or a supposed celebration of a
Life.
People gathered in and dispersed out:
Like leaves in a restless wind,
Close relatives, lifelong friends and acquaintances,
In a strange dance of
Morbidity.
Respectful, dignified,
The funeral structure
To be observed rigidly
At all costs.
But I left, wondering
Would the deceased have wanted it,
As sad and distant as this?

The Papers Were Read

The papers were read.
To no one who cared,
Only for the fee.
Grey suited men and neat precise ladies.
Would have heard
To empty walls.
The end of an impossible
Loving dream world.
We both participated in and destroyed
Without even realising
Why.
We let it all slip away.
No protests of any passion.
No historical mention
 of loving years together.
Playing at a spinster
You could never be
Kept me at a distance.
The papers were read
To no one who cared a
Hoot.
Terse official words
Describing inadequately a tragedy.
Neither one of us
Would ever be quite
The same.

The Reality of a Sudden Wooden Maiden

Can you see her?
She's a glimpse of a wink
And half as pink.
Beneath the leafy undergrowth
And crunchy branches.
She strolls and woos you.
Between your looking
Aside and behind.
She`s a glimpse and a wink.
Maybe she's real
And half as pink.
Can you see her?
Can you see you?
She strokes your head
And swings into her dream.
She strolls and woos you.
Between alert eyes,
And suspense or fear.
Amidst leafy undergrowth
and crunchy branches.
Watching from her perch.
What is she?
Is she you?
She strokes your hand,
And trips your feet
As you nervously laugh
Into deadly stillness.

The Subject is Taboo

Walked the streets of the dead,
Where legendary gods have rallied and bled,
For causes too fine for mere mortals
To comprehend.
The subject is taboo,
Of the night of long knives
Running you through.
The subject really is taboo.
If death was a soldier, a mercenary blue
If death was a railroad where
Everyone shuffles through.
The subject really is rather taboo.
If dead was alive
And people survived
What could we make of this
Momentary glimpse?
It really is rather quaint
This taboo.

To Old Lovers Anywhere

I am miles away,
Like an old dearly loved obscure song.
A different town, a different time,
Do not look the same,
Only worse,
The high street would say.
I am miles away!
Not the same person you cared for.
Our little niche was then.
Tucked away in cupboards
Photos and love poems discarded.
Materials of long ago.
I drive in a car like a lost soul.
Looking for a kindred spirit.
Fearful of another lightless winter.
Waiting for a ship called destiny,
Not seen around here lately.

Tumbleweed Chalet

There it was
A paraffin coloured shack,
All locked up and black.
Hidden amongst the trees.
A sort of don't you see me.
But the river gave it
A mild reflection
And the fishermen
Were half-dozing
In the midday sun.
It's the son of
Tumbleweed chalet.
Just like the old days.
I dreamt I was
A cowboy.
Leaning on its boardwalk.
Further on I went
Into the weeds.
Half a dozen ghost towns
Strangled and forgotten please.
By council demand-
This land is private!
My feet fell through
Fallen canvas ceilings,
That lay upon the floor.
It's the son
Of a tumbleweed chalet,
And maybe,

I am the valet
Or the wild cat
That darts in and out.
Half a broken gate
Leads to another
Ruin innate.
Punctured mattresses,
Cracked glass,
Daubed walls,

Turned over tables.
By council demand!
This land is private
And overrun!!!

Type to Type

Type to type
They walked off into
The night
As irritated as youth.
Contemplative, yet certain
Of desire.
This life of chance and nonsense,
Of other worlds and
Sliding outcomes.
Amidst casual
Disassociation.
Type to type
Of now.
No different
Than of youth of mine.
Different tools of assembly,
Result the same.

Uncomfortable

I'm driving out in the countryside.
This country.
Uncomfortable,
With my fellow humankind.
If we aren't emphasising
Difference of colour
We are
Finding fault in others.
But never analysing
Our shortcomings,
As human beings.
Uncomfortable.
Betrayed, uncomfortable
With our unbalanced media.
Uncomfortable,
With our failing democratic politic.
Let it breathe,
 Don't sheath it
With paranoia.
Uncomfortable, oh so
Uncomfortable.
I am driving back home
In the country.
Our country, my country.
On a dank night.
Wondering if we are
Heading for a
New dawn or recycled persecution.

"Weekends"

I feel Friday's impatience
Roaring in cold engines,
Hate rev-ving and storing.

We Kissed

We kissed and kissed,
But never stayed together.

We longed and longed,
Always promising to make it better.

You Cannot do Anything Without Love.

You cannot do anything without love.
You cannot do anything.
Cannot get up in the morning.
You cannot do anything without love.
All momentum is change.
I cannot help feeling,
Love is the power of everything.
And you cannot feel anything without love.
Hate drains you by the second.
You cannot do anything without love.
You cannot do.
You cannot do.
I cannot help feeling,
Love is the power of everything.
Fortune and coincidence,
They are often misinterpreted.
Fate is the hidden hand.
Even the hardest heart
Cannot survive without love.
You cannot do,
You just cannot do.

www.ingramcontent.com/pod-product-compliance
Lightning Source LLC
Chambersburg PA
CBHW020950090426
42736CB00010B/1356